This book is dedicated to

Evie- Layla

Written by
Kayleigh Jane Smith

Illustrated by:
Nagy Iby
&
Kayleigh Jane Smith

Edited By
Hailey Peterson

There once was a little girl named Evie who was no bigger than a cat, but she was as brave as a lion.

Every morning, Evie would look out the window into the garden and see the birds, bees, and other beings all living together in harmony.

One morning, Evie's mother fell asleep with the window open.

Without hesitation, Evie made her way towards the window as quick as she could. Once Evie reached the window ledge, she did not know what to do next. But then, out of nowhere, a friendly face appeared. It was Rikki!

Rikki was Evie's best friend. Her fur was as soft as silk, and her whiskers were as poised as the queen's guards. Her tail was as long as a magical wand.

Rikki hunched down so Evie could climb on her back. Evie climbed up and Rikki yelled, "Hold on!" before leaping off the window ledge and landing in the tall grass below.

Evie jumped off Rikki's back and headed straight towards the big gum tree at the bottom of the garden.

Before Evie could ask any questions, Rikki jumped over the fence and was gone as quickly as she appeared

After a short minute, Evie heard a little voice say: "Hey! Aren't you that little girl who lives inside the window?"

Evie looked all around. "Who said that?!"

"Down here!" replied the voice. "This is the thing with you humans. We're all around you but you don't pay attention!"

Then, in the sniff of a cat's whisker, a tiny beetle flew onto the tip of Evie's nose.

"Hi!"

Evie paused, wondering if she had indeed gone mad.

"Well, aren't you going to say hello back?!" said the beetle.

"Hi?! I'm Evie. What's your name?"

"Barry," the beetle replied.

"Nice to meet you, Barry. I sure do envy you and your easy life out here!"

"Oh, Evie, it's quite the opposite! We beetles are very busy. We have a very important job here on this planet. We live all over the world. We come in different shapes and sizes, but we all have the same job. We all help the planet stay beautiful by cleaning it every day. We eat things like rotting wood, leaves, and other nasty bits.

Byeee!

"The next time you come outside and see how beautiful the planet is, just say, 'Thank you, beetles, for keeping the planet so beautiful!'"

And with that, he flew away.

Evie looked around and noticed the fresh smell of the flowers. She said, "Thank you, beetles, for keeping the planet so beautiful!"

Evie crawled through the grass. It wasn't long until she was greeted by a group of worms. She had never seen a worm before, and at first she thought, "My, what ugly things!"

Before Evie could say a word, the worms said, "Hello, Evie! We are so happy to finally meet you!"

"How do you know my name?" replied Evie.

"Well, Evie, we are always around. You humans are just too distracted to notice! People don't usually talk to us much because of how we look, but we are kind, and we have a great job.

"We are earthworms. We are here to help protect the planet too, Evie, just like all the other bugs and insects. It's our job to eat the organic materials in the soil to recycle the nutrients! This is a very important job!"

I did not know that..

Before Evie could ask any questions, the worms yelled "CROW!!!!" and disappeared under the soil.

Evie looked around and
noticed how colourful the
garden was. She said,
"Thank you, worms, for
keeping the planet so
beautiful!"

With that, a crow landed on the ground near Evie. "Drat, it looks like I was too slow this time!"

"Hi, I'm Evie!"

"Yes, yes, I know who you are, You can call me Ms Crow" she replied as she hopped through the tall grass and scanned the ground for bugs.

Back away, nice and slowly...

"Ms. Crow, do you also have a job in the world?"

"Yes, little Evie. Every living being has a very important job here in the world! Although we crows do have a taste for fresh crops, we also eat a lot of the garbage that is created by humans each year. We help prevent the spread of nasty smells and we even help keep humans from feeling unwell.

"So, the next time you come outside, Evie, and see how beautiful the planet is, just say, 'Thank you, crows, for keeping the planet so beautiful!'"

Then, just like that, she flew away.

Evie looked around and appreciated how clean the garden looked She said, "Thank you, crows, for keeping the planet so beautiful!"

Evie then crawled some more until she reached the gigantic gum tree at the bottom of the garden. She began to climb it.

Evie climbed and climbed until she reached a sturdy branch. She decided to stop for a rest.

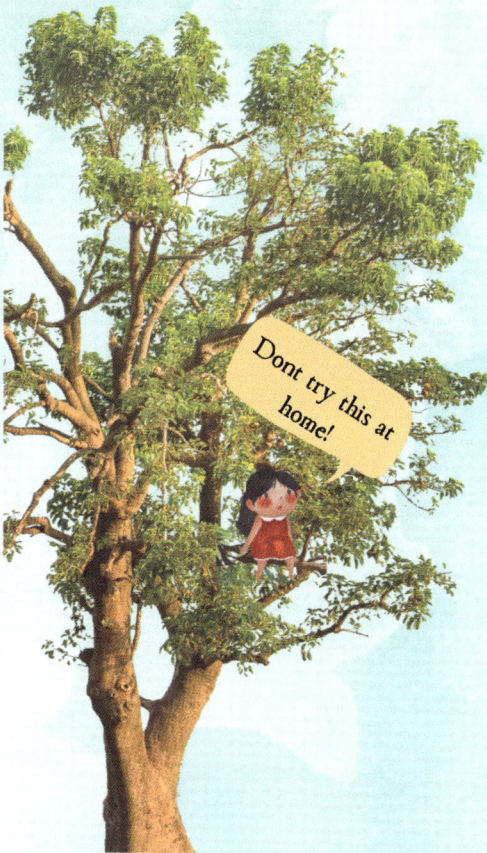

As Evie rested on the
tree branch, as she
looked around she saw a
big spider sitting on the
branch right next to her!

Before she could make a noise, the spider smiled and said, "Don't be afraid, little Evie! I mean you no harm! We spiders are more afraid of you than you are of us!

"Please, call me Harriet! Harriet Huntsman. The name is much scarier than we actually are. There are some spiders out there that can give you a nasty nip, so always be careful. You don't have to fear us, we are peaceful creatures who have a very important job, little Evie. We spiders have the important job of keeping the insect population at a steady number, including those pesky flies and mosquitos who like to turn up to your picnics uninvited and give you a little nibble."

"So, the next time you come outside, Evie, just say, 'Thank you, spiders, for keeping the planet so beautiful!'"

And just like that, the spider crawled away.

Evie looked around and noticed how fresh the air smelt. She said, "Thank you, spiders, for keeping the planet so beautiful!"

As Evie sat in the tree, she heard a very familiar buzzing sound.. Before she could look to see where it was coming from, a mosquito flew right up to Evie's face.

As Evie went to swat the mosquito away, the mosquito yelled "Relax, relax! Moss is the name"

I'm not here to bite you, I'm here to set a few things straight, little Evie!

"I couldn't help but overhear a few things Harriet Huntsman said. Although what she said is true, we are not just biting bugs, little Evie! I know we aren't very popular, but still, we have a very important job.

Typical Harriet

"We mosquitos help pollinate plants and flowers, which is vital to the ecosystem.

"So, the next time you come outside, Evie, just say, 'Thank you, mosquitos, for keeping the planet so beautiful!'" And just like that, the mosquito flew away.

Evie looked around and noticed that all the plants were looking so vibrant and green. She said, "Thank you, mosquitos, for keeping the planet so beautiful!"

After a rest, Evie decided to climb a little bit
further up the tree. She climbed and climbed
until she reached a very busy branch.

This branch was busy with bees. This time,
the bees did not come over to Evie. They
were all working hard as they flew around
Evie yelling,

"Excuse me, coming through!"
"Coming through! Don't mind me."
"Beg your pardon, Evie!"

Hey Honey!

Evie followed the bees and saw the most beautiful beehive she had ever seen. Inside, there was one very relaxed-looking bee who was different from the others.

"Hello, Evie," said the bee. "Welcome to my hive. I am the queen bee, but you can call me Queenie.

Apologies that my bees haven't had time to talk to you, Evie, but we work non-stop!"

"What do you do?" asked Evie.

"Well, we are hard at work all day. We pollinate plants and flowers so that new ones can grow to replace them and produce oxygen.

"Although we have stingers on us, we do not want to use them.

"So, the next time you step outside, Evie, just say, 'Thank you, bees, for keeping the planet so beautiful!'"

And just like that, Queenie went straight back to work in the hive.

I've forgotten my keys again

BUSY

Evie realised she was starting to get tired, so
she decided it was time to go back inside.

As Evie began to crawl back down the tree,
she heard a loud rustling sound...

She looked over and saw a koala in the tree
yawning and stretching.

G'Day

"Good morning, Evie! Another beautiful day, isn't it? I couldn't help but overhear my friend's teaching you about all their jobs,

Karls the name.

"Although us Koala's sleep most of the day, we eat the excess vegetation that would otherwise end up on forest floors while, This helps prevent bushfires from getting more fuel and getting bigger.

Evie then noticed how tall all the trees were and how their lush leaves rustled in the warm breeze. She said, "Thank you, koalas, for keeping the planet so beautiful!"

That's a nice breeze..

Evie realised she was ready for a nap too. She decided to continue climbing back down the tree.

As she crawled back through the garden, she had a new appreciation for all the bugs she once thought were yucky. She now knew that the bugs, insects, and animals all worked hard to keep the planet beautiful.

As Evie reached the window Rikki reappeared. Evie leapt onto Rikki's back and held on tight as Rikki jumped up onto the window ledge. Before Evie crawled back inside the window, she turned around to face the garden and said;

"Thank you, friends in the garden, for keeping the planet so beautiful!"

So next time you see a friend in the garden, just say thank you friends, for keeping the planet so beautiful.

Maybe I'll get some lines in the next book?

Printed in Great Britain
by Amazon